THE SCIENCE OF GETTING RICH

T0145571

THE SCIENCE OF GETTING RICH

by Wallace D. Wattles

*The Legendary Mental Program
to Wealth and Mastery*

Abridged and Introduced
by Mitch Horowitz

THE CONDENSED CLASSICS LIBRARY™

MEDIA

Published by Gildan Media LLC
aka G&D Media.
www.GandDmedia.com

The Science of Getting Rich was originally published in 1910
G&D Media Condensed Classics edition published 2018
Abridgement and Introduction copyright © 2016 by Mitch
Horowitz

FIRST EDITION: 2018

Cover design by David Rheinhardt of Pyrographx

Interior design by Meghan Day Healey of Story Horse, LLC.

ISBN: 978-1-7225-0058-0

Contents

The Ethic of Success

Some people have deeply contradictory feelings about the idea of "getting rich." They believe that getting rich sounds gauche, unspiritual, or selfish. This book by American social reformer and New Thought pioneer Wallace D. Wattles will put those mixed feelings to rest.

Wattles, a fighter for progressive causes as well as a pioneering mind theorist, believed that the true aim of enrichment was not the mere accumulation of personal resources, but the establishment of a better world: a world of shared abundance and possibility for all people.

His guidebook *The Science of Getting Rich* was obscure until about ten years ago. In 2007, word spread that *The Science of Getting Rich* was a source behind the mega-selling book and movie *The Secret*. The book began to hit bestseller lists, nearly than a century after

the author's death in 1911. I published an edition my-
self that reached number-one on the *Businessweek* bestseller list.

But what many of Wattles's new generation of read-
ers missed was his dedication to the ethic of collective
advancement and creativity above animal competition;
his belief that competition itself was an outmoded idea,
soon to be supplanted but the creative capacities found
within the mind. And that once unlocked, these higher
capacities would grant working men and women the
keys to a life of prosperity for themselves and for all
around them.

Was his vision really so utopian? We live in an age
of remarkable advances in placebo studies, extending
even to "placebo surgery" and mentally based weight-
loss; new findings in the field called neuroplasticity,
which show that the brain's neural pathways are literally
"rewired" by habits of thought; extraordinary questions
posed by quantum physics experiments, which suggest
causality between thought and object; and ongoing and
serious experiments in ESP, which repeatedly demonstrate some kind of nonphysical conveyance of data in
laboratory settings.

Wattles's vision, now more than a century old, was
simply to ask whether these remarkable abilities, which
were only hinted at in the science labs of his day, could

be applied and experimented with on the material scale of daily life.

Wattles did not live long enough to see the influence of his book. He died of tuberculosis less than a year after it appeared. But his calm certainty and profoundly confident yet gentle tone suggest that he understood the portent of what he was writing.

Like every great thinker, Wattles left us not with a doctrine, but rather with articles of experimentation. The finest thing you can do to honor the memory of this good man—and to advance your own place in life—is to heed his advice: Go and experiment. Go and try. And if you experience results, as I think you will, do what he did: Tell the people.

—Mitch Horowitz

CHAPTER ONE

For Those Who Want Money

This book is a practical manual, not a treatise upon theories. It is intended for men and women whose most pressing need is money; who wish to get rich first, and philosophize afterward. It is for those who have, so far, found neither the time, the means, nor the opportunity to go deeply into the study of metaphysics, but who want results and who are willing to take the conclusions of science as a basis for action, without going into all the processes by which those conclusions were reached.

It is expected that the reader will take the fundamental statements of this book upon faith; and, taking the statements upon faith, that he will prove their truth by acting upon them without fear or hesitation.

Every man or woman who does this will certainly get rich; for the science herein is an exact science, and failure is impossible. For the benefit, however, of those who wish to investigate philosophical theories and secure a logical basis for faith, I will here cite certain authorities.

The monistic theory of the universe—the theory that One is All, and that All is One; that one Substance manifests itself as the seeming many elements of the material world—is of Hindu origin, and has been gradually winning its way into the thought of the western world for two hundred years. It is the foundation of all the Oriental philosophies, and of those of Descartes, Spinoza, Leibnitz, Schopenhauer, Hegel, and Emerson.

In writing this book I have sacrificed all other considerations to plainness and simplicity of style, so that all might understand. The plan of action laid down herein was deduced from the conclusions of philosophy; it has been thoroughly tested, and bears the supreme test of practical experiment: *it works*. If you wish to know how the conclusions were arrived at, read the writings of the authors mentioned above; and if you wish to reap the fruits of their philosophies in actual practice, read this book, and do exactly as it tells you to do.

Chapter Two

The Right to be Rich

The object of life is development; and everything that lives has an inalienable right to all the development that it is capable of attaining.

Man's right to life means his right to have the free and unrestricted use of all things necessary to his fullest mental, spiritual, and physical unfoldment; or, in other words, his right to be rich.

In this book, I do not speak of riches in a figurative way; to be really rich does not mean to be satisfied or contented with a little. No man ought to be satisfied with a little if he is capable of using and enjoying more. The purpose of Nature is the advancement and unfoldment of life; and every man should have all that can contribute to the power, elegance, beauty, and richness of life. To be content with less is sinful.

The desire for riches is really the desire for a richer, fuller, and more abundant life.

There are three motives for which we live: the body, the mind, and the soul. No one of these is better or holier than the other; all are alike desirable, and no one of the three—body, mind, or soul—can live fully if either of the others is cut short of full life and expression.

Real life means the complete expression of all that man can give forth through body, mind, and soul.

Wherever there is unexpressed possibility, or function not performed, there is unsatisfied desire. Desire is possibility seeking expression, or function seeking performance.

It is perfectly right that you should desire to be rich; if you are a normal man or woman you cannot help doing so. It is perfectly right that you should give your best attention to the Science of Getting Rich, for it is the noblest and most necessary of all studies. If you neglect this study, you are derelict in your duty to yourself, to God and humanity; for you can render to God and humanity no greater service than to make the most of yourself.

CHAPTER THREE

There Is a Science of Getting Rich

There is a Science of Getting Rich, and it is an exact science, like algebra or arithmetic. There are certain laws that govern the process of acquiring riches.

The ownership of money and property comes as a result of doing things in a *certain way*; those who do things in this Certain Way, whether on purpose or accidentally, get rich; while those who do not do things in this Certain Way, no matter how hard they work or how able they are, remain poor.

The ability to do things in this certain way is not due solely to birth or talent, for many people who have great talent remain poor, while others who have little talent get rich.

Studying the people who have gotten rich, we find that they are an average lot in all respects, having no greater talents and abilities than other men. It is evident that they do not get rich because they possess talents and abilities that other men have not, but because they happen to do things in a Certain Way.

Some degree of ability to think and understand is, of course, essential; but insofar as natural ability is concerned, any man or woman who has sense enough to read and understand these words can get rich.

It is true that you will do best in a business that you like, and that is congenial to you; and if you have certain talents that are well developed, you will do best in a business that calls for those talents.

Also, you will do best in a business that is suited to your locality; an ice-cream parlor would do better in a warm climate than in Greenland, and a salmon fishery will succeed better in the Northwest than in Florida, where there are no salmon.

But, aside from these general limitations, getting rich is not dependent upon your engaging in some particular business, but upon your learning to do things in a Certain Way that causes success. It is this to which we now turn.

CHAPTER FOUR

Is Opportunity Monopolized?

It is quite true that if you are a workman in the employ of the steel trust you have very little chance of becoming the owner of the plant for which you work; but it is also true that if you will commence to act in a Certain Way, you can soon leave the employ of the steel trust for new opportunity.

At different periods the tide of opportunity sets in different directions, according to the needs of the whole, and the particular stage of social evolution that has been reached.

There is abundance of opportunity for the man who will go with the tide, instead of trying to swim against it.

The workers are not being "kept down" by their masters. As a class, they are where they are because they do not do things in a Certain Way. If the workers of America chose to do so, they could follow the example of their brothers in Belgium and other countries, and establish great department stores and co-operative industries; they could elect men of their own class to office, and pass laws favoring the development of such co-operative industries; and in a few years they could take peaceable possession of the industrial field.

The working class may become the master class whenever they will begin to do things in a Certain Way; the law of wealth is the same for them as it is for all others. This they must learn; and they will remain where they are as long as they continue to do as they do. The individual worker, however, is not held down by the ignorance or the mental slothfulness of his class; he can follow the tide of opportunity to riches.

The visible supply is practically inexhaustible; and the invisible supply really IS inexhaustible.

Everything you see on earth is made from one original substance, out of which all things proceed.

New forms are constantly being made, and older ones are dissolving; but all are shapes assumed by One Thing.

There is no limit to the supply of Formless Stuff, or Original Substance. The universe is made out of it; but it was not all used in making the universe. The spaces in, through, and between the forms of the visible universe are permeated and filled with the Original Substance; with the formless Stuff; with the raw material of all things. Ten thousand times as much as has been made might still be made, and even then we should not have exhausted the supply of universal raw material.

Nature is an inexhaustible storehouse of riches; the supply will never run short. Original Substance is alive with creative energy, and is constantly producing more forms. When the supply of building material is exhausted, more will be produced; when the soil is exhausted so that foodstuffs and materials for clothing will no longer grow upon it, it will be renewed or more soil will be made. When all the gold and silver has been dug from the earth, if man is still in such a stage of social development that he needs gold and silver, more will produced from the Formless. The Formless Stuff responds to the needs of man; it will not let him be without any good thing.

The Formless Stuff is intelligent; it is stuff that thinks. It is alive, and is always impelled toward more life.

It is the natural and inherent impulse of life to seek to live more; it is the nature of intelligence to enlarge itself, and of consciousness to seek to extend its boundaries and find fuller expression. The universe of forms has been made by Formless Living Substance, throwing itself into form in order to express itself more fully.

The universe is a great Living Presence, always moving inherently toward more life and fuller functioning.

Nature is formed for the advancement of life; its impelling motive is the increase of life. For this cause, everything that can possibly minister to life is bountifully provided; there can be no lack unless God is to contradict himself and nullify his own works.

I shall demonstrate shortly that the resources of the Formless Supply are at the command of the man or woman who will act and think in a Certain Way.

CHAPTER FIVE

The First Principle in the Science of Getting Rich

Thought is the only power that can produce tangible riches from the Formless Substance. The stuff from which all things are made is a substance that thinks, and a thought of form in this substance produces the form.

Original Substance moves according to its thoughts; every form and process you see in nature is the visible expression of a thought in Original Substance. As the Formless Stuff thinks of a form, it takes that form; as it thinks of a motion, it makes that motion. That is the way all things were created. We live in a thought world, which is part of a thought universe. The thought of a moving universe extended throughout Formless Substance, and the Thinking Stuff moving according to that thought, took the form of systems of planets, and maintains that form. Thinking Substance takes the form of its thought, and moves according to the thought.

Every thought of form held in thinking Substance, causes the creation of the form but always, or at least generally, along lines of growth and action already established.

No thought of form can be impressed upon Original Substance without causing the creation of the form.

Man is a thinking center, and can originate thought. All the forms that man fashions with his hands must first exist in his thought; he cannot shape a thing until he has thought that thing.

Yet so far man has confined his efforts wholly to the work of his hands; he has applied manual labor to the world of forms, seeking to change or modify what already exists. He has never thought of trying to cause the creation of new forms by impressing his thoughts upon Formless Substance.

As our first step, we must lay down three fundamental propositions:

1) There is a thinking stuff from which all things are made, and which, in its original state, permeates, penetrates, and fills the interspaces of the universe.

2) A thought, in this substance, produces the thing that is imaged by the thought.

3) Man can form things in his thought, and, by impressing his thought upon formless substance, can cause the thing he thinks about to be created.

Read these creed statements over and over again; fix every word upon your memory, and meditate upon them until you firmly believe what they say.

There is no labor from which most people shrink as they do from that of sustained and consecutive thought; it is the hardest work in the world. This is especially true when truth is contrary to appearances. Every appearance in the visible world tends to produce a corresponding form in the mind that observes it; and this can be prevented only by holding the thought of the TRUTH.

Do not ask why these things are true, nor speculate as to how they can be true; simply take them on trust.

The science of getting rich begins with the absolute acceptance of this faith.

CHAPTER SIX

Increasing Life

The desire for riches is simply the capacity for larger life seeking fulfillment; every desire is the effort of an unexpressed possibility to come into action. It is power seeking to manifest that causes desire. That which makes you want more money is the same as that which makes the plant grow: it is Life, seeking fuller expression.

The One Living Substance must be subject to this inherent law of all life; it is permeated with the desire to live more; that is why it is under the necessity of creating things.

It is the desire of God that you should get rich. He wants you to get rich because He can express himself better through you if you have plenty of things to use in giving Him expression. He can live more in you if you have unlimited command of the means of life.

The universe desires you to have everything you want to have.

Nature is friendly to your plans.

Everything is naturally for you.

Make up your mind that this is true.

It is essential, however that *your purpose should harmonize with the purpose that is in All.*

You must want real life, not mere pleasure of sensual gratification. Life is the performance of function; and the individual really lives only when he performs every function, physical, mental, and spiritual, of which he is capable, without excess in any.

Remember, however, that the desire of Substance is for all, and its movements must be for more life to all; it cannot be made to work for less life to any, because it is equally in all, seeking riches and life.

Intelligent Substance will make things for you, but it will not take things away from some one else and give them to you.

You are to become a creator, not a competitor; you are going to get what you want, but in such a way that when you get it every other man will have more than he has now.

I am aware that there are men who get a vast amount of money by proceeding in direct opposition to the statements above, and may add a word of explanation here. Men of the plutocratic type, who become very rich, do so sometimes purely by their extraordinary ability on the plane of competition; and sometimes they unconsciously relate themselves to Substance in its great purposes and movements for the general racial upbuilding through industrial evolution. Rockefeller, Carnegie, Morgan, et al., have been the unconscious agents of the Supreme in the necessary work of systematizing and organizing productive industry; and in the end, their work will contribute immensely toward increased life for all. Their day is nearly over; they have organized production, and *will soon be succeeded by the agents of the multitude, who will organize the machinery of distribution.*

The multi-millionaires are like the monster reptiles of the prehistoric eras; they play a necessary part in the evolutionary process, but the same Power that produced them will dispose of them. And it is well to bear in mind that they have never been really rich; a record of the private lives of most of this class will show that they have really been the most abject and wretched of the poor.

Riches secured on the competitive plane are never satisfactory and permanent; they are yours today, and another's tomorrow. Remember, if you are to become rich in a scientific and certain way, you must rise entirely out of the competitive thought.

Let us consider once more:

There is a thinking stuff from which all things are made, and which, in its original state, permeates, penetrates, and fills the interspaces of the universe.

A thought, in this substance, produces the thing that is imaged by the thought.

Man can form things in his thought, and, by impressing his thought upon formless substance, can cause the thing he thinks about to be created.

The supply is limitless.

CHAPTER SEVEN

How Riches Come to You

When I say that you do not have to drive sharp bargains, I do not mean that you do not have to drive any bargains at all, or that you are above the necessity for having any dealings with your fellow men. I mean that you will not need to deal with them unfairly; you do not have to get something for nothing, *but can give to every man more than you take from him.*

You cannot give every man more in cash market value than you take from him, but you can give him more in use value than the cash value of the thing you take from him. The paper, ink, and other material in this book may not be worth the money you pay for it; but if the ideas suggested by it bring you thousands of dollars, you have not been wronged by those who sold it to you; they have given you a great use value for a small cash value.

Give every man more in use value than you take from him in cash value; then you are adding to the life of the world by every business transaction.

If you have people working for you, you must take from them more in cash value than you pay them in wages; but you can so organize your business that it will be filled with the principle of advancement, and so that each employee who wishes to do so may advance a little every day.

You can make your business do for your employees what this book is doing for you. You can so conduct your business that it will be a sort of ladder, by which every employee who will take the trouble may climb to riches himself; and given the opportunity, if he will not do so it is not your fault.

CHAPTER EIGHT

Gratitude

The whole process of mental adjustment and atonement can be summed up in one word: gratitude.

First, you believe that there is one Intelligent Substance, from which all things proceed; second, you believe that this Substance gives you everything you desire; and third, you relate yourself to it by a feeling of deep and profound gratitude.

Many people who order their lives rightly in all other ways are kept in poverty by their lack of gratitude. Having received one gift from God, they cut the wires that connect them with Him by failing to make acknowledgment.

It is easy to understand that the nearer we live to the source of wealth, the more wealth we shall receive; and it is easy also to understand that the soul that is always grateful lives in closer touch with God than the one that never looks to Him in thankful acknowledgment.

The more gratefully we fix our minds on the Supreme when good things come to us, the more good things we will receive, and the more rapidly they will come; and the reason simply is that the mental attitude of gratitude draws the mind into closer touch with the source from which the blessings come.

There is a Law of Gratitude, and it is absolutely necessary that you should observe the law, if you are to get the results you seek.

The Law of Gratitude is the natural principle that action and reaction are always equal, and in opposite directions.

The grateful outreaching of your mind in thankful praise to the Supreme *is a liberation or expenditure of force; it cannot fail to reach that to which it addressed, and the reaction is an instantaneous movement towards you.*

"Draw nigh unto God, and He will draw nigh unto you." That is a statement of psychological truth.

CHAPTER NINE

Thinking in a Certain Way

I t is not enough that you should have a general desire for wealth "to do good." Everybody has that desire.

It is not enough that you should have a wish to travel, see things, live more, etc. Everybody has those desires, too. If you were going to relay a radio message to a friend, you would not send the letters of the alphabet in their order, and let him construct the message for himself; nor would you take words at random from the dictionary. You would send a coherent sentence; one that meant something.

When you try to impress your wants upon Substance it must be done by a coherent statement; you must know what you want, and be definite. You can never get rich, or start the creative power into action, by sending out unformed longings and vague desires.

You must have a clear mental picture continually in mind, and you must keep your face toward it all the time.

It is not necessary to take exercises in concentration, nor to set apart special times for prayer and affirmation. These things are well enough, but all you need is to know what you want, and to want it badly enough so that it will stay in your thoughts.

Spend as much of your leisure time as you can in contemplating your picture, but no one needs to take exercises to concentrate his mind on a thing that he really wants; it is the things you do not really care about that require effort to focus upon.

The more clear and definite you make your picture then, and the more you dwell upon it, bringing out all its delightful details, the stronger your desire will be; and the stronger your desire, the easier it will be to hold your mind fixed upon the picture of what you want.

Something more is necessary, however, than merely to see the picture clearly.

Behind your clear vision must be the purpose to realize it; to bring it out in tangible expression.

And behind this purpose must be an invincible and unwavering FAITH that the thing is already yours; that it is "at hand" and you have only to take possession of it.

Live in the new house, mentally, until it takes form around you physically. In the mental realm, enter at once into full enjoyment of the things you want.

"Whatsoever things ye ask for when ye pray, believe that ye receive them, and ye shall have them," said Jesus.

You do not need to pray repeatedly for things you want; it is not necessary to tell God about it every day.

"Use not vain repetitions as the heathen do," Jesus told his pupils, "for your Father knoweth that ye have need of these things before ye ask Him."

Your part is to intelligently formulate your desires for the things which make for a larger life, and to get these desires arranged into a coherent whole; and then to impress this Whole Desire upon the Formless Substance, which has the power and the will to bring you what you want.

You do not make this impression by repeating strings of words; you make it by holding the vision with unshakable PURPOSE to attain it, and with steadfast FAITH that you do attain it.

The answer to prayer is not according to your faith while you are talking, but according to your faith while you are working.

CHAPTER TEN

How to Use the Will

To set about getting rich in a scientific way, do not try to apply your will power to anything outside of yourself.

You have no right to, anyway.

It is wrong to apply your will to other men and women in order to get them to do what you wish done.

It is as flagrantly wrong to coerce people by mental power as it is to coerce them by physical power. If compelling people by physical force to do things for you reduces them to slavery, compelling them by mental means accomplishes the same thing.

You have no right to use your will power upon another person, even "for his own good;" for you do not know what is for his good.

To get rich, you need only to use your will power upon yourself.

When you know what to think and do, then you must use your will to compel yourself to think and do the right things. That is the legitimate use of the will in getting what you want—to use it in holding yourself to the right course. Use your will to keep yourself thinking and acting in the Certain Way.

Do not try to project your will, or your thoughts, or your mind out into space, to "act" on things or people.

Keep your mind at home; it can accomplish more there than elsewhere.

Use your mind to form a mental image of what you want, and to hold that vision with faith and purpose; and use your will to keep your mind working in the Right Way.

The more steady and continuous your faith and purpose, the more rapidly you will get rich, because you will make only POSITIVE impressions upon Substance; and you will not neutralize or offset them by negative impressions.

The picture of your desires, held with faith and purpose, is taken up by the Formless. As this impression spreads, all things are set moving toward its realization; every living thing, every inanimate thing, and the things yet uncreated, are stirred toward bringing into being that which you want. All force begins to be exerted in that direction; all things begin to move toward you. The minds of people, everywhere, are influenced toward doing the things necessary to the fulfilling of your desires; and they work for you, unconsciously.

Since belief is all-important, it behooves you to guard your thoughts; and as your beliefs will be shaped to a very great extent by the things you observe and think about, it is important that you should command your attention.

Chapter Eleven

Further Use of the Will

You cannot retain a true and clear vision of wealth if you are constantly turning your attention to opposing pictures, whether they are external or imaginary.

Do not tell of your past troubles of a financial nature; if you have had them, do not think of them at all. Do not tell of the poverty of your parents, or the hardships of your early life; to do any of these things is to mentally class yourself with the poor for the time being, and it will certainly check the movement of things in your direction.

"Let the dead bury their dead," as Jesus said.

Put poverty and all things that pertain to poverty completely behind you.

You have accepted a certain theory of the universe as being correct, and are resting all your hopes of happiness on its being correct; and what can you gain by giving heed to conflicting theories?

You can aim at nothing so great or noble, I repeat, as to become rich; and you must fix your attention upon your mental picture of riches, to the exclusion of all that may tend to dim or obscure the vision.

You must learn to see the underlying TRUTH in all things; you must see beneath all seemingly wrong conditions the Great One Life ever moving forward toward fuller expression and more complete happiness.

The very best thing you can do for the whole world is to make the most of yourself.

CHAPTER TWELVE

Acting in the Certain Way

This is the crucial point in the Science of Getting Rich—right here, where thought and personal action must be combined. Many people, consciously or unconsciously, set the creative forces in action by the strength and persistence of their desires, yet they remain poor because they do not provide for the reception of the thing they want when it comes.

By thought, the thing you want is brought to you; by action you receive it.

Whatever your action is to be, it is evident that you must act NOW. You cannot act in the past, and it is essential to the clearness of your mental vision that you dismiss the past from your mind. You cannot act in the future, for the future is not here yet. And you cannot tell how you will want to act in any future contingency until that contingency has arrived.

Because you are not in the right business, or the right environment now, do not think that you must postpone action until you get into the right business or environment. And do not spend time in the present taking thought as to the best course in possible future emergencies; have faith in your ability to meet any emergency when it arrives.

Put your whole mind into present action.

Do not bother as to whether yesterday's work was well done or ill done; do to-day's work well.

Do not try to do tomorrow's work now; there will be plenty of time to do that when you get to it.

Do not try, by occult or mystical means, to act on people or things that are out of your reach.

Do not wait for a change of environment, before you act; get a change of environment by action.

You can so act upon the environment in which you are now, as to cause yourself to be transferred to a better environment.

Hold with faith and purpose the vision of yourself in the better environment, but act upon your present environment with all your heart, and with all your strength, and with all your mind.

You can advance only by being larger than your present place; and no man is larger than his present place who leaves undone any of the work pertaining to that place.

Doing what you want to do is life; and there is no real satisfaction in living if we are compelled to be forever doing something that we do not like to do. And it is certain that you can do what you want because the *desire* to do it is proof that you have within you the power that *can* do it.

Desire is a manifestation of power.

The desire to play music is the power that can play music seeking expression and development.

If there are past mistakes whose consequences have placed you in an undesirable business or environment, you may be obliged for some time to do that which you do not like to do; but you can make the doing of it pleasant by knowing that it is making it possible for you to come to the doing of what you want to do.

Remember always that definiteness of purpose, the ability of your thoughts to impress themselves upon the great Original Substance of the universe, the sincere impulse toward creative function, the desire to build—not to best—your neighbor, and the dedication to doing all you can wherever you are, place at your back an awesome power of Truth, to which nothing can be denied.

Build the world that you dream of for yourself and others; bring prosperity and beauty into creation; improve yourself—and you improve the world. That is the noblest goal to which any man or woman can aspire.

About the Authors

A progressive social reformer and New Thought pioneer, WALLACE D. WATTLES was born in 1860 in the United States. He popularized creative-thought principles in his groundbreaking classics *The Science of Getting Rich, The Science of Being Great,* and *The Science of Being Well.* A great influence on future generations of success writers, he died in 1911.

MITCH HOROWITZ, who abridged and introduced this volume, is the PEN Award-winning author of books including *Occult America* and *The Miracle Club: How Thoughts Become Reality. The Washington Post* says Mitch "treats esoteric ideas and movements with an even-handed intellectual studiousness that is too often lost in today's raised-voice discussions." Follow him @MitchHorowitz.

Printed in the USA
CPSIA information can be obtained
at www.ICGtesting.com
JSHW012047140824
68134JS00034B/3299

9 781722 500580